Everyday Spelling
Book 2

Elske Brown and Judy Jackson

OXFORD

UNIVERSITY PRESS

Contents

Introduction		*3*
Unit 1	sh	4
Unit 2	a–e	6
Unit 3	th	8
Unit 4	i–e	10
Unit 5	ck	12
Unit 6	ar	14
Unit 7	o–e	16
Unit 8	ow	18
Unit 9	*Review*	20
Unit 10	Stepping up	22
Unit 11	ng	24
Unit 12	oo	26
Unit 13	ee	28
Unit 14	ea	30
Unit 15	ch	32
Unit 16	oo	34
Unit 17	ow	36
Unit 18	ai	38
Unit 19	*Review*	40
Unit 20	Stepping Up	42
Unit 21	oa	44
Unit 22	or	46
Unit 23	ll, ss, tt, nn	48
Unit 24	dd, pp, bb, rr	50
Unit 25	ou	52
Unit 26	air	54
Unit 27	aw	56
Unit 28	ew	58
Unit 29	*Review*	60
Unit 30	Stepping up	62
Unit 31	ir	64
Unit 32	y	66
Unit 33	er	68
Unit 34	ur	70
Unit 35	ea	72
Unit 36	oi	74
Unit 37	ay	76
Unit 38	o	78
Unit 39	en	80
Unit 40	*Review*	82
Unit 41	Stepping up	84
Alphabetical list		86

Introduction

Everyday Spelling is a series of six student textbooks. Each book is a year's work based on 41 units. This includes four review units and four two-page challenge units entitled 'Stepping up'. The units are based around a word list. The words used are those that the children should be familiar with and are likely to use in their writing. A variety of activities involves the children writing the words to reinforce correct spelling as well as encouraging the development of a broader vocabulary. Each unit in Book 2 consists of two pages.

Look, Cover, Write, Check
1 LOOK: Children study the word
2 COVER: Children cover the word so that it is hidden
3 WRITE: Children write the word
4 CHECK: Children check to see the word is correct. If not, they repeat the process above.

The *Everyday Spelling* books provide a cover flap for this process.

LIST WORDS

In Book 2, the word list at the beginning of each unit consists of:
• eight letter-family group words
• two commonly-used words or demons
• two interest words
• space for children's personal words

REVIEW UNITS

Units 9, 19, 29, and 40 are review units. The activities review a selection of words that focus on sounds from the previous units. These activities will test the children's knowledge and understanding of the relevant spelling concepts and vocabulary. These units may be used as tests to indicate individual strengths, or where additional work may be useful.

STEPPING UP

These four, two-page units contain challenging activities. The activities in these units are geared to extend the more competent students.

ALPHABETICAL LIST

Included at the back of the book is an alphabetical list of words used in the Unit lists.

sh

ship	*Ship*
shed	*Shed*
brush	*brush*
crush	*crush*
fresh	*fresh*
splash	*splash*
shape	*shape*
shoe	*shoe*

Footwear

boots	*boots*
runners	*runners*

Common words

blue	*blue*
true	*true*

My words

shelby   *shiny*

Unit 1

I **brush** my **shoes** to make them shiny.

☆ Write the list words into the correct shapes.

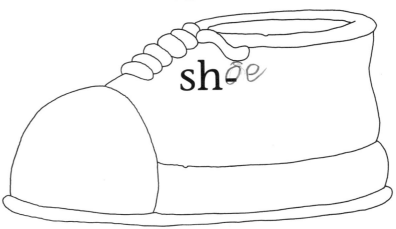

sh*oe*

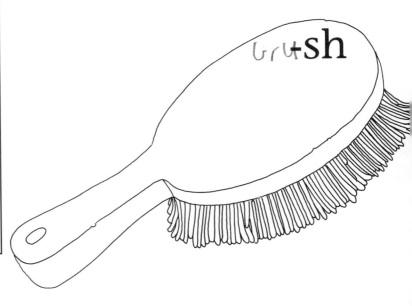

*bru*sh

☆ Write the list words that have these words in them.

he	*shed*	hip	*ship*	hoe	*shoe*
ash	*splash*	boot	*boots*	rush	*brush*
run	*runners*	ape	*shape*		*sh shelby*

4

⭐ **Unjumble the list words and write them correctly.**

crush — uchrs

blue — ulbe

shed — sdhe

true — ture

splash — lsapsh

fresh — refhs

shape — asehp

boots — bstoo

⭐ **Trace and add ue.**

tr u e   bl u e   gl u e
cl u e   S u e   resc u e

⭐ **Write a ue word for each clue.**

1 A girl's name   S u e

2 To stick something   g l u e

3 A colour   b l u e

4 Something to help find the answer   c l u e

5 To save someone   r e s c u e

6 Something that is real   t r u e

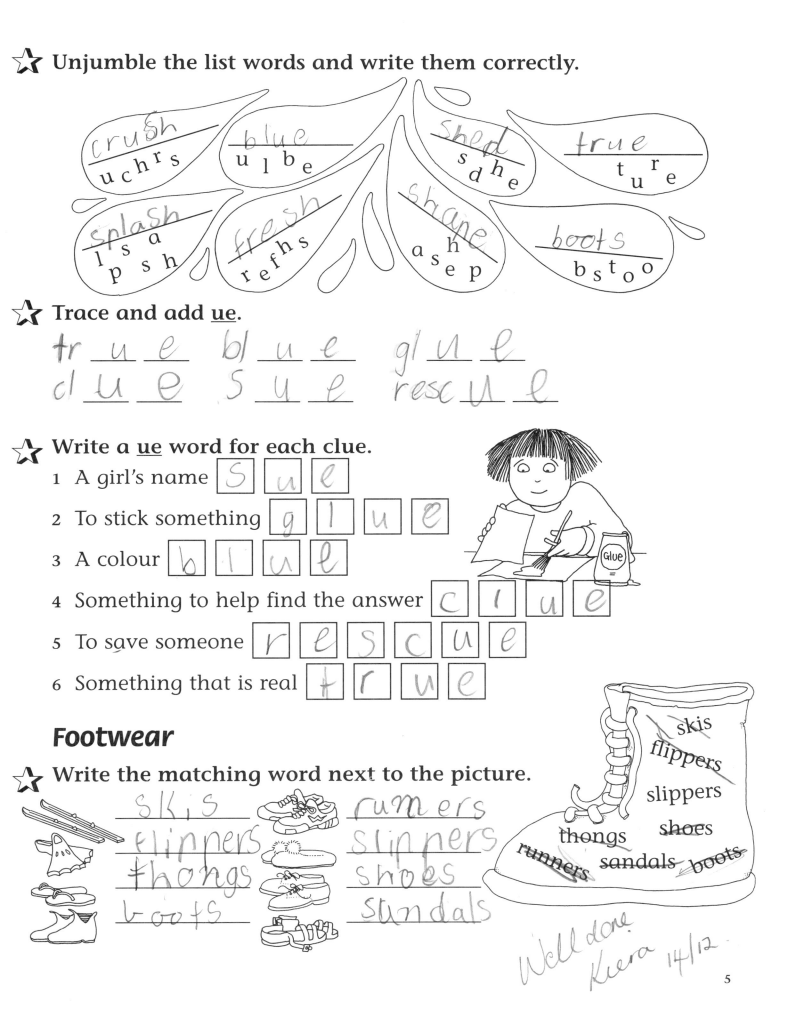

Footwear

⭐ **Write the matching word next to the picture.**

skis   runners

flippers   slippers

thongs   shoes

boots   sandals

Word bank (on boot): skis, flippers, slippers, shoes, thongs, sandals, boots, runners

Well done.
Keira 14/12

5

a–e

make — *make*

came — *came*

cake — *cake*

take — *take*

made — *made*

game — *game*

name — *name*

spade — *spade*

Computer games

computer — *computer*

mouse — *mouse*

Common words

race — *race*

later — *later*

My words

_____ _____

Unit 2

My **name** is _Kiera_

⭐ Trace and complete each list word.

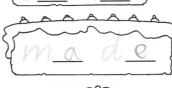
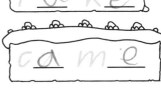

cake *take*

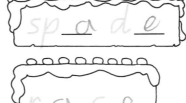

made *came*

spade *game*

race *make*

When <u>e</u> is added to some short <u>a</u> words, it gives the word a long <u>a</u> sound. Example: <u>mat</u> becomes <u>mate</u>.

⭐ Write the long <u>a</u> words.

can + e = *cane*

tap + e = *tape*

hat + e = *hate*

⭐ Draw a line from the short <u>a</u> and long <u>a</u> matching pictures.

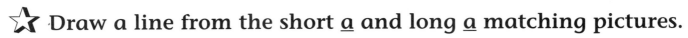
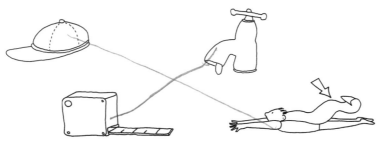

6

⭐ **Fill the gap with <u>ate</u> 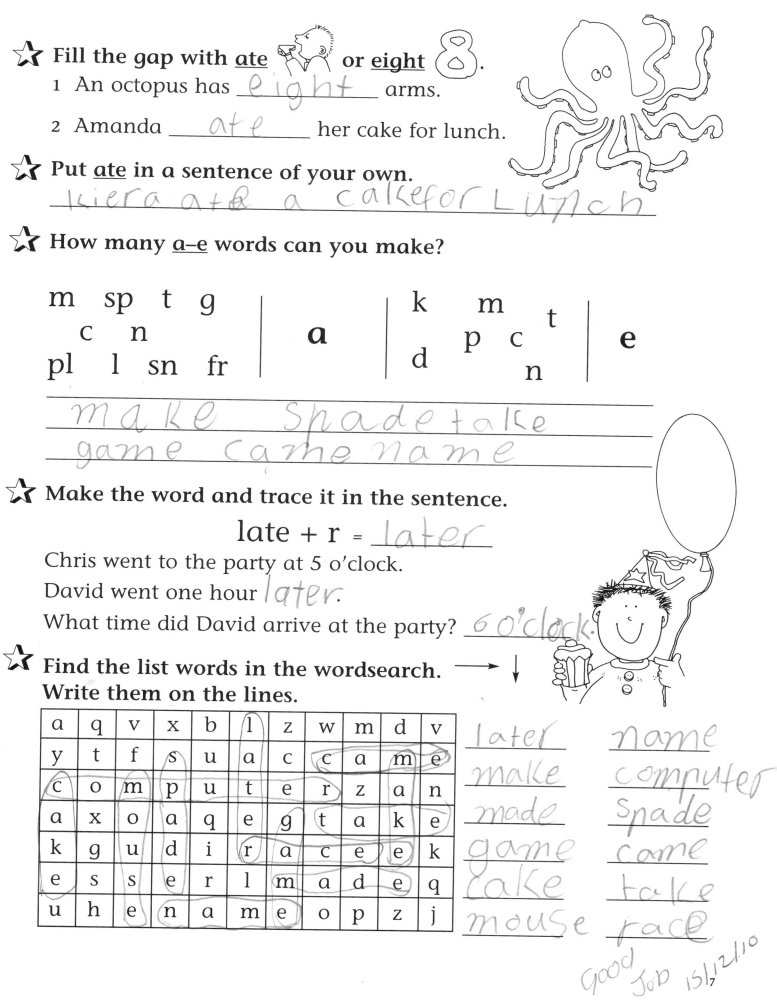 or <u>eight</u> 8.**

1 An octopus has ___eight___ arms.

2 Amanda ___ate___ her cake for lunch.

⭐ **Put <u>ate</u> in a sentence of your own.**

___Kiera ate a cakefor Lunch___

⭐ **How many <u>a–e</u> words can you make?**

m sp t g		k m t	
c n	**a**	p c	**e**
pl l sn fr		d n	

___make spade take___
___game came name___

⭐ **Make the word and trace it in the sentence.**

late + r = ___later___

Chris went to the party at 5 o'clock.

David went one hour _later._

What time did David arrive at the party? ___6 o'clock.___

⭐ **Find the list words in the wordsearch.** → ↓
Write them on the lines.

a	q	v	x	b	l	z	w	m	d	v
y	t	f	s	u	a	c	c	a	m	e
c	o	m	p	u	t	e	r	z	a	n
a	x	o	a	q	e	g	t	a	k	e
k	g	u	d	i	r	a	c	e	e	k
e	s	s	e	r	l	m	a	d	e	q
u	h	e	n	a	m	e	o	p	z	j

later   name
make   computer
made   spade
game   came
cake   take
mouse   race

good job 15/12/10

th

then	*then*
them	*them*
this	*this*
with	*with*
think	*think*
throw	*throw*
thirteen	*thirteen*
Numbers	
eleven	*eleven*
twelve	*twelve*
Common words	
there	*there*
their	*their*

My words

that   *t*

Unit 3

Some people **think** that **thirteen** is an unlucky number.

☆ **Make the th words.**

th + is = *this*

th + ink = *think*

th + row = *throw*

wi + th = *with*

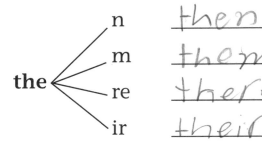

the
- n — *then*
- m — *them*
- re — *there*
- ir — *their*

☆ **Write the list words with these words in them.**

it *with*   hen *then*

row *throw*   here *there*

his *this*   even *eleven*

☆ **Fill the gap with a list word.**

1 The number after twelve is *thirteen*.

2 Adam can *throw* a ball very fast.

3 Yes, you can go with *them* to the shops.

4 Come and play *with* us.

5 *this* is my dog.

Use **there** when you mean a place. Example: over **there**.
Use **their** when you mean belonging to them. Example: **their** coats.

☆ **Colour the correct box.**

1 We went | their | there | last week.

2 They put | their | there | hats on.

☆ **Find the small words in:**

their _____ _____   there _____ _____ _____ _____

☆ **Write the answers in number words.**

1 Twelve plus one equals _12 + 1 = 13_ .

2 Thirteen take away two equals _13 - 2 = 11_ .

3 Eleven plus one equals _11 + 1 = 12_ .

☆ **Rewrite the list words by adding the vowels (a e i o u).**

thn	thrw	ths	wth	thnk	thrtn
then	throw	this	with	think	thirteen

thr	twlv	thm	lvn
there	twelve	them	eleven

Wordsearch → ↓ ↑

☆ **Find all the list words. Colour each one in a different colour. Write each word as you find it.**

think   there   then

throw   their   them

with   this   _____

_____   thirteen

b	r	c	t	d	a	e	t
f	i	t	h	e	n	g	h
h	e	l	e	v	e	n	i
t	h	i	r	t	e	e	n
h	t	s	e	h	i	v	k
r	j	i	k	e	l	l	m
o	n	h	o	m	p	e	q
w	i	t	h	r	s	w	t
u	w	y	z	a	b	t	c

9

i–e

kite   *Kite*

ride   *ride*

bike   *bike*

mine   *mine*

nice   *nice*

rice   *rice*

slide   *slide*

stripe   *stripe*

Numbers

nineteen   *ninteen*

ninety   *ninety*

Common words

live   *live*

white   *white*

My words

_____ _____

Unit 4

Slide down the slide and have a **nice ride**.

⭐ **Trace and complete the list words.**

nice
stripe
mine
live
rice
white
ninety
nineteen

When e̱ is added to some short i̱ words, it makes a long i̱ sound. Example: hi̱d becomes hi̱de.

⭐ **Write the long i̱ words.**

rid + e = *ride*

kit + e = *kite*

slid + e = *slide*

strip + e = *stripe*

bit + e = *bite*

rip + e = *ripe*

⭐ **Circle the words with the long i̱ sound.**

mine   fine   shin   fin

shine   pipe

time   pip   white   wipe

⭐ Colour the correct word in each row to match the picture.

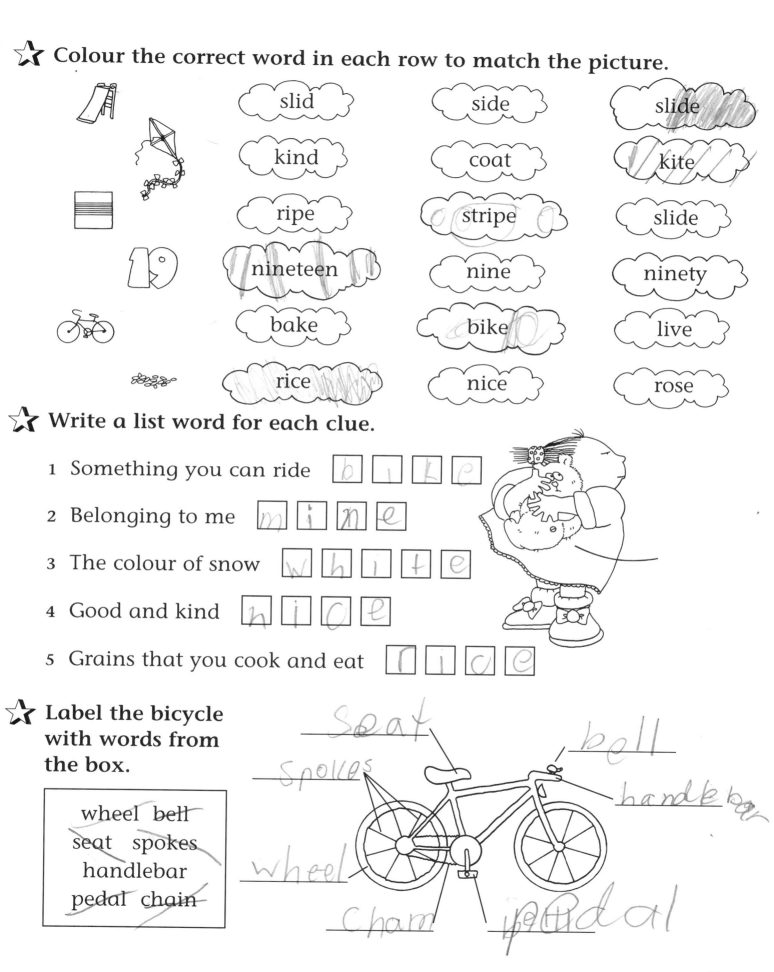

slid	side	**slide**
kind	coat	**kite**
ripe	**stripe**	slide
nineteen	nine	ninety
bake	**bike**	live
rice	nice	rose

⭐ Write a list word for each clue.

1 Something you can ride b i k e

2 Belonging to me m i n e

3 The colour of snow w h i t e

4 Good and kind n i c e

5 Grains that you cook and eat r i c e

⭐ Label the bicycle with words from the box.

wheel bell
seat spokes
handlebar
pedal chain

seat
bell
spokes
handlebar
wheel
chain pedal

11

ck

neck _____

truck _____

track _____

stick _____

quack _____

o'clock _____

jacket _____

packet _____

Time

half _____

past _____

Common words

what _____

colour _____

My words

_____ _____

Unit 5

The **truck** will deliver the **packet**s of chips at **half past** eleven.

⭐ **Write the ck words in the truck.**

truck   book   half

rocket   colour   block

snack   jacket   o'clock

quack

stick

what   packet   track   neck

picnic   past   call   was

⭐ **Change one letter in each word to make a new word.**

1 Change **quick** to a noise a duck makes. _____

2 Change **stack** to something you do with glue. _____

3 Change **trick** to a railway line. _____

4 Change **click** to something that tells the time. _____

12

⭐ Trace the words and colour the picture.

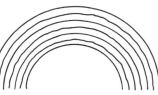

What colour

is a leaf?

What colour

is a banana?

What colour

is an apple?

What colour

is a rainbow?

⭐ Complete and draw the pictures.

jack + *et* = _____

pack + *et* = _____

rock + *et* = _____

What time is it?

⭐ Write the times the clocks show.

_____

_____

_____

⭐ Show your own o'clock and half-past times. Write them.

_____

_____

_____

⭐ On a piece of paper write two meanings for the word <u>stick</u>.
Use a dictionary to help you.

ar

bark _____

dark _____

hard _____

start _____

party _____

carpet _____

market _____

garden _____

Outside

plant _____

backyard _____

Common words

do _____

doing _____

My words

_____ _____

Mary **plant**ed a **garden** of pretty flowers in her **backyard**.

☆ **Colour the flowers that have an _ar_ word.**

for

girl

half

plant

backyard

start

short

garden

frown

party

dark

market

hard

bark

track

carpet

past

☆ **Match the list words to the shapes.**

☆ Write the **ing** words.

do
be ⟶ **ing**
go

_____

_____

_____

☆ Fill the gap with **do** or **doing**.

1 I can _____ my shoelaces up.

2 They are _____ their shoelaces up.

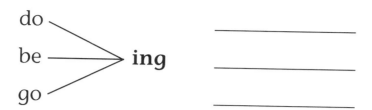

☆ Put these words in sentences.

dark _____

plant _____

party _____

☆ Write a list word for each clue to find the mystery word.

1 A dog does this

2 The beginning of a race

3 Something soft that covers the floor

4 A place to buy fruit and vegetables

5 You might have this on your birthday

6 Something that grows in the garden

7 Opposite of soft

8 Where flowers grow

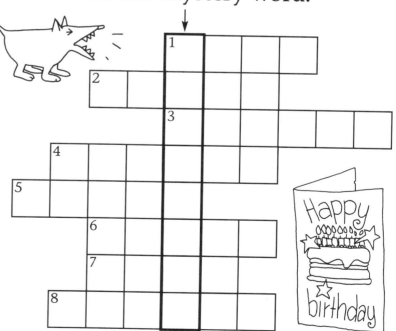

The mystery word is _____

15

o–e

bone   _____

note   _____

rope   _____

hope   _____

cone   _____

woke   _____

drove   _____

chose   _____

Writing

pencil   _____

paper   _____

Common words

open   _____

close   _____

My words

_____   _____

When **e** is added to some short **o** words, it gives the word a long **o** sound. Example: **not** becomes **note**

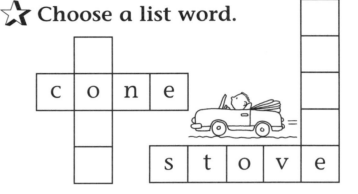

Unit 7

EXCURSION **NOTE**
Please bring **pencil** and **paper**.

Rhyming words

⭐ Choose a list word.

⭐ **Circle the words with a long <u>o</u> sound.**

not   note   hope   hop   rod   rode
drove   bone   frog   lost   stone   rope
cone   close   block   chose

16

⭐ **Rewrite each sentence with the correct words from the brackets.**

1 I (hop, hope) that it will not rain.

_____

2 Dad wrote a (rope, note) to my teacher.

_____

3 Mary (chose, close) pink (pencil, paper) to make a birthday card.

_____

_____

 Write the list word.

             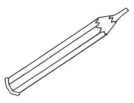

_____   _____   _____   _____   _____

⭐ **Write the opposite for each word from the box.**

open – _____   up – _____

soft – _____   more – _____

hello – _____   long – _____

hard	less
down	goodbye
short	close

⭐ **Change a letter to make a new word. Read the clues.**

1 none – _____ (a number)

2 hose – _____ (a flower)

3 come – _____ (used for your hair)

 Draw pictures to show two meanings for <u>close</u>.

OW

now   _____

how   _____

down   _____

howl   _____

growl   _____

frown   _____

crowd   _____

flower   _____

In the jungle

animal   _____

wild   _____

Common words

they   _____

because   _____

My words

_____   _____

Unit 8

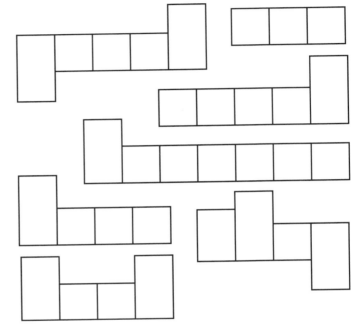

We could hear the **wild animal howl** in the night.

⭐ **Match list words to the shapes.**

⭐ **Fill the gap with flour** 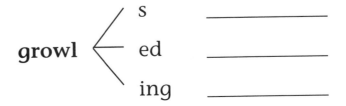 **or flour** .

1   I picked a _____ from the garden.

2   We used two cups of _____ to make a cake.

⭐ **Write the ow words.**

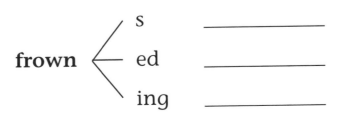

frown ← s _____
        ed _____
        ing _____

growl ← s _____
        ed _____
        ing _____

⭐ **Follow the trail and write a list word for each clue.**

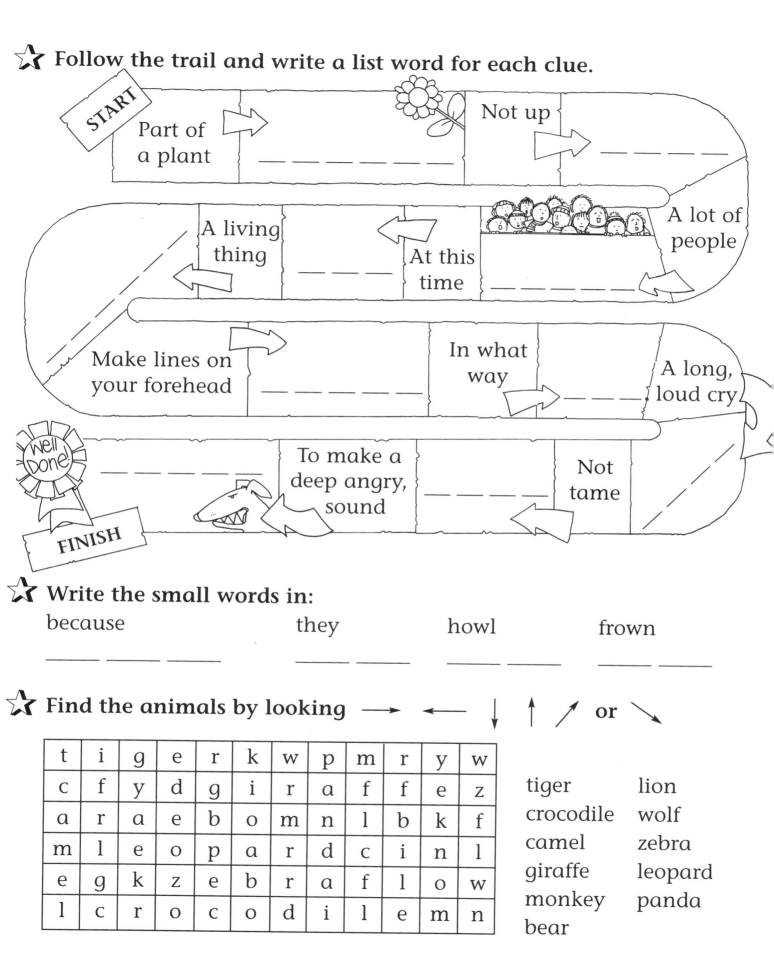

START

Part of a plant _ _ _ _ _ _

Not up _ _ _ _ _

A lot of people _ _ _ _ _ _

At this time _ _ _ _

A living thing _ _ _ _ _ _

Make lines on your forehead _ _ _ _ _

In what way _ _ _

A long, loud cry _ _ _ _ _

To make a deep angry, sound _ _ _ _ _

Not tame _ _ _ _

Well Done!

FINISH _ _ _ _ _ _ _

⭐ **Write the small words in:**

because _ _ _ _ _ _ _

they _ _ _ _

howl

frown

⭐ **Find the animals by looking** → ← ↓ ↑ ↗ **or** ↘

t	i	g	e	r	k	w	p	m	r	y	w
c	f	y	d	g	i	r	a	f	f	e	z
a	r	a	e	b	o	m	n	l	b	k	f
m	l	e	o	p	a	r	d	c	i	n	l
e	g	k	z	e	b	r	a	f	l	o	w
l	c	r	o	c	o	d	i	l	e	m	n

tiger   lion
crocodile   wolf
camel   zebra
giraffe   leopard
monkey   panda
bear

Unit 9 Review

⭐ Choose a word from the kite to rhyme with each word.
Add one more of your own.

quack _____

_____

sink _____

_____

smoke _____ _____

down _____ _____

(kite with words:) name slide dark track stick frown think woke

game _____ _____

pick _____ _____

hide _____ _____

bark _____ _____

⭐ How many words can you make?

b		m		a		t		n		
	c				i					e
sl	r	n		o		d	k			

_____

_____

_____

→ 10 good
11 → 18 great
19 → fantastic!

⭐ Colour the box with the correct word.

1 The | trick | truck | was full of rocks.

2 Fried | rice | mice | is yummy to eat.

3 A | mouse | house | is used with a computer.

4 Please | open | close | the door behind you.

5 Let's go to the | garden | market | to buy some food.

6 I | think | thank | we can | how | throw | the ball
over | their | there | .

⭐ Write each word in the correct picture.

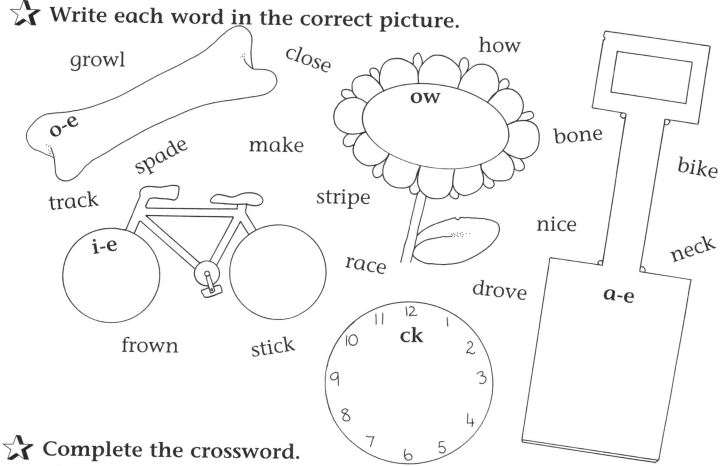

growl close how

o-e ow bone

spade make bike

track stripe nice neck

i-e race a-e

drove

frown stick ck

⭐ Complete the crossword.

There is a sound clue in brackets after each word.

Across

1 Opposite to black (i-e)
5 At this time (ow)
7 Something you do your hair with (–sh)
9 I can ___ this crossword
10 Opposite to close
11 What you are called (a-e)
12 Part of your body (ck)

Down

2 Rhymes with cow (ow)
3 Number after twelve (th)
4 Where flowers grow (ar)
6 A large boat (sh–)
8 Dogs like to chew this (o-e)

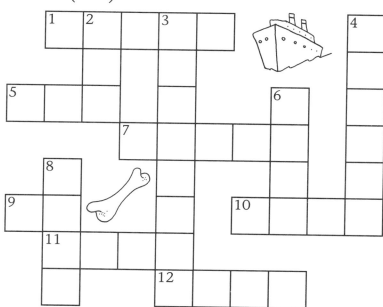

Unit 10 Stepping up

Connecting up the computer

⭐ Label the computer with the words on the disc.

keyboard

mouse

hard drive

cable

speaker

printer

monitor

Now write the words on the screen in alphabetical order.

There, their or they're

⭐ Make the words.

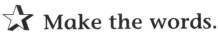

th

ere ___there___ —means in that place. I live over <u>there</u>.

eir _____ —means belonging to them. <u>Their</u> bikes are new.

y're _____ —means 'they are'. <u>They're</u> going on camp.

Fill the gap.

_____ lining up over _____ where _____ team is.

You be the editor

Help Emma edit her e-mail by circling the 20 misspelt words.
Write the correct spelling on the lines below.

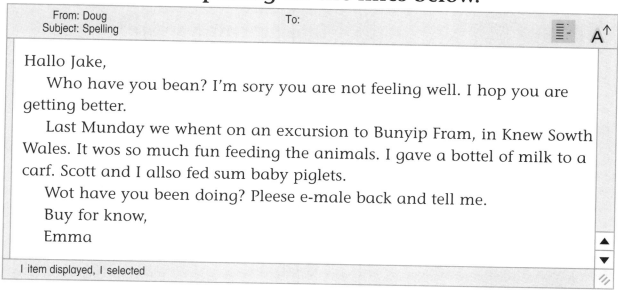

From: Doug
Subject: Spelling
To:

Hallo Jake,

Who have you bean? I'm sory you are not feeling well. I hop you are getting better.

Last Munday we whent on an excursion to Bunyip Fram, in Knew Sowth Wales. It wos so much fun feeding the animals. I gave a bottel of milk to a carf. Scott and I allso fed sum baby piglets.

Wot have you been doing? Pleese e-male back and tell me.

Buy for know,

Emma

I item displayed, I selected

_____

_____

_____

A cricket wicket!

Make the words _____

_____ _____

_____ _____

_____ _____

pa   ti   po

bu   cri   ro

ja   ra   wi

ck   et

Match a –cket word from above with each clue.

1 Something you can wear.   _____

2 This can go to the moon.   _____

3 Jack and Jill had one.   _____

4 Chips can come in this.   _____

5 You need this to get into a movie.   _____

6 A loud noise   _____

7 A sport.   _____

8 A coat has this to put things in.   _____

9 Another word for cricket stumps.   _____

ng

rang _____

bang _____

along _____

strong _____

string _____

spring _____

stung _____

belong _____

Baby animals

lamb _____

kitten _____

Common words

going _____

morning _____

My words

_____ _____

Unit 11

The **lamb** was born early one **morning** in **spring**.

⭐ **Write the list words for the clues.**

1 very thin rope

— — — — — —

2 a loud noise

— — — —

3 bitten

— — — — —

4 before noon

— — — — — — —

5 powerful

— — — — — —

6 a young sheep

— — — —

7 a young cat

— — — — — —

8 to be owned by someone

— — — — — —

⭐ **Add _ing_ to each word to make a new word.**

jump _jumping_   belong _____

play _____   bang _____

sing _____   want _____

Write the words.

h	f	b
s	**ang**	
	r	g

_____   _____

_____   _____

_____   _____

Choose an <u>ang</u> word.

The bell _____ at nine o'clock.

	s	
l	**ong**	g
al	th	str

_____   _____

_____   _____

_____   _____

Choose an <u>ong</u> word.

We walked _____ the bush track.

 Write the matching baby animals.

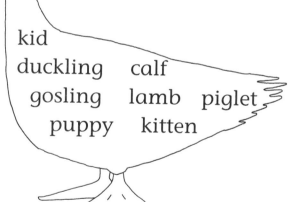

cat _____   dog _____

pig _____   sheep _____

duck _____   cow _____

goat _____   goose _____

kid
duckling   calf
gosling   lamb   piglet
puppy   kitten

 Match the different meanings of <u>spring</u> to the pictures with a line.

1 A season

2 Water coming from the ground

3 A coil of wire

4 To jump up

oo

zoo   _____

too   _____

food   _____

roof   _____

cool   _____

broom   _____

spoon   _____

school   _____

The zoo

kangaroo   _____

koala   _____

Common words

I'm   _____

it's   _____

My words

_____   _____

Unit 12

At the **zoo** we saw a **kangaroo**, a **koala**, a wombat and an emu **too**.

⭐ **Write the list words inside the kangaroo.**

wood   book

broom   roof   foot

wool

school

spoon

took

food

good

cool

Two, to or too?

My friend is coming **too**.

two

To the beach

Too big!

⭐ **Fill the gaps.**

1 We walked _____ the park.

2 Our family has _____ cars.

3 My sister has a bike. I have one _____.

4 It is _____ cold to go to the pool today.

⭐ **Colour the correct box.**

1 The baby ate her | roof | food | with a | spoon | soon | .

2 Most of the children in our grade go to | school | cool | by car.

3 | I'm | I'll | going to my friend's place.

4 We are going to the | zoo | cool | | moon | soon | .

⭐ **Write the words you coloured on the line.**

_____

Contractions

An apostrophe (') is used to show that one or more letters have been left out. Example: is n~~o~~t = isn't

⭐ **Write the contractions to match the words.**

I am _____   it is _____

do not _____   did not _____

he is _____   can not _____

Contractions	
don't	he's
can't	I'm
it's	didn't

⭐ **Label the Australian animals.**

possum   platypus   dingo   kangaroo

kookaburra   wombat   koala   emu

_____	_____	_____	_____
_____	_____	_____	_____

ee

bee	_____
meet	_____
feed	_____
deep	_____
week	_____
sleep	_____
teeth	_____
queen	_____
Numbers	
fourteen	_____
fifteen	_____
Common words	
were	_____
where	_____
My words	
_____	_____

Unit 13

Did you know?
A **queen bee** can sting without dying.

☆ **Complete the list words.**

_ _ _ _ _   _ _ _ _ _

_ _ _   _ _ _ _ _

_ _ _ _ _ _ _ _   _ _ _ _

_ _ _ _ _

☆ **Write the compound words.**

some + where = _____

any + where = _____

☆ **Choose _were_ or _where_ to fill each gap.**

1 I do not know _____ my bag is.

2 The children _____ playing outside.

3 Our teeth _____ checked by the dentist.

4 _____ did you put the book?

Write the ee list words for the clues.

1 Seven days
2 A flying insect
3 She wears a crown
4 A long way down
5 Deep rest
6 You should brush these
7 Eat or give food
8 Come together

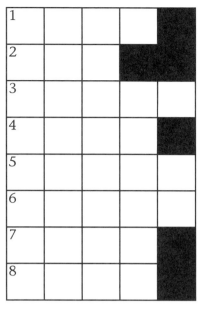

Words that sound the same

meet   meat

bee   be

wear   where

Sunday, Monday . . .

week

weak

Not strong

Where are you?
Are you here or are you there?

 Circle the correct word.

1 Kerryn was stung on the foot by a (be, bee).
2 Dad cooked the (meet, meat) on the barbecue.
3 My friend will (meet, meat) me at the swings.
4 I will (wear, where) my new shoes today.
5 There are seven days in one (weak, week).

⭐ **Write your own sentence for <u>be</u>.**

_____

⭐ **Write the number words (under twenty) that have <u>ee</u>.**

_____

_____

ea

meal _____

seat _____

real _____

team _____

hear _____

near _____

year _____

teacher _____

Teams

sport _____

basketball _____

Common words

here _____

want _____

My words

_____ _____

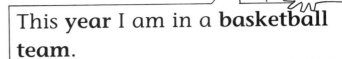

Unit 14

This **year** I am in a **basketball team**.

⭐ **Unjumble the list words in the basketballs.**

_____   _____

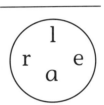

_____   _____

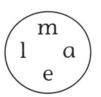

_____   _____

_____   _____

I am here.

I **hear** with my **ear**.

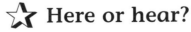

⭐ **Here or hear?**

1 I can _____ a dog barking.

2 Your mother is _____.

30

a b c d e f g h i j k l m n o p q r s t u v w x y z

⭐ **Write each line of words in alphabetical order.**

1 year   here   basketball   meal

_____

2 seat   want   teacher   hear

_____

⭐ **Write the smaller words in:**

seat   want   hear   team   beach

_____   _____   _____   _____   _____

_____   _____   _____   _____   _____

_____

⭐ **Cross out the word that does not belong.**
Write it on the line.

1 year   month   seat   day   _____

2 meal   bench   chair   seat   _____

3 doctor   teacher   dentist   year   _____

4 hear   see   feel   team   _____

5 speak   talk   dream   say   _____

6 meat   banana   peach   apple   _____

7 basketball   near   tennis   soccer   _____

⭐ **Which sport? Label the pictures.**

| | | | | tennis |
| football |
| basketball |

_____   _____   _____

ch

such   _____

bench   _____

bunch   _____

punch   _____

each   _____

peach   _____

pinch   _____

cheer   _____

Fruit salad

apple   _____

pear   _____

Common words

which   _____

witch   _____

My words

_____   _____

Unit 15

| Apples, pears and peaches are healthy fruit to eat. |

⭐ Trace and add <u>ch</u> to each word.

⭐ Use <u>an</u> before words starting with a vowel (<u>a e i o u</u>). Write <u>a</u> before words starting with a consonant.

_____ apple   _____ grape   _____ pear   _____ banana

_____ orange   _____ egg   _____ peach   _____ onion

32

☆ Fill the gaps with a list word or one from the banana. Use the picture clues to help.

banana fruit lunch cheese sandwich

Cameron sat down on the _____ _____ to eat his _____. He had a _____ _____, a _____ _____ slice and some _____ salad. In _____, a _____ fruit salad there was an _____, a _____, a _____ a _____, and some _____.

of

☆ ...lete the table.

	Add **ed**	Add **ing**
pinch	_____	_____
punch	_____	_____
cheer	_____	_____

☆ Use **which** or **witch** to complete the sentences.

1 The _____ wore a long, black cloak.

2 _____ football team do you barrack for?

☆ **Which** **witch** has an **itch**? Use the code to find the answer.

___ ___ ___   ___ ___ ___ ___   ___   ___ ___ ___ ___ ___ ___
20 8 5   23 9 20 3   8   5 1 20 9 14 7

___   ___ ___ ___ ___ ___ ___ ___ ___ ___.
 1   19 1 14 4 23 9 3 8.

oo

wood _____

hook _____

hoof _____

hood _____

stood _____

looked _____

cooking _____

goodbye _____

What's cooking?

bowl _____

flour _____

Common words

would _____

could _____

My words

_____ _____

The fish ~~oo~~ked at the **hook.** he get caug~~ld~~

Goodbye. You won't catch me!

☆ **Write list words for the pictures.**

_____ _____

See you later

_____ _____

_____ _____

_____ _____

_____ _____

_____ _____

☆ **Complete each word for these clues.**

~~P~~art of a horse's foot   ☐ oo ☐

~~so~~mething to go over your head   ☐ oo ☐

~~so~~mething to mix a cake in   ☐ ow ☐

~~___~~ is used in cooking   ☐ ☐ ou ☐

☆ **Make the words and complete the sentences.**

c —
w —⟩ould

_____

_____

1 We _____ like to go on a bike ride.

2 _____ we go bowling, please?

☆ **Write the words with the same oo sound in the correct picture.**

hook	zoo	too	cook	school	look	wood
roof	hood	food	spoon	good	took	boot

☆ **Colour the correct box.**

1 They | looks | looked | for the lost ball.

2 We are | cooking | cooked | a cake for tea.

3 Go and find some | would | wood | for the fire.

4 | Flown | Flour | is made from wheat.

5 I | stood | stand | under the umbrella when it rained.

☆ **Draw the two meanings for bowl. Use your dictionary to help you.**

35

OW

own _____

slow _____

blow _____

glow _____

grown _____

know _____

arrow _____

window _____

Measuring

metre _____

litre _____

Common words

put _____

home _____

My words

_____ _____

Did you **know**?
The largest marrow **grown** weighed 61.23 kg.

☆ **Colour over the x's. Rewrite the letters that are left to find a list word.**

xoxxwxnx _____

bxxlxoxw _____

xarxxrow _____

xgxlxowx _____

sxlxoxwx _____

xxknxoxw _____

wxindxow _____

mextxrxe _____

gxroxwnx _____

☆ **Find the small words in:**

know _____ _____

grown _____ _____ _____

window _____ _____

_____ _____

a b c d e f g h i j k l m n o p q r s t u v w x y z

☆ **Write a list word that starts with the letter that comes before:**

t _slow_

m _____

n _____

x _____

l _____

p _____

36

☆ **Fill in the missing letters.**

put   p __ t   __ ut   __ __ t   pu __   __ u __

☆ **Circle the correct word.**

1 Please (pull, put) the book in your bag.

2 Drew can (put, putt) his own shoes on.

☆ **Fill in the missing letters.**

home   h __ me   h __ m __   __ __ m __   __ __ __ e

☆ **Draw a line between the pictures in the box and their correct homes. Label each home with a word from the box below.**

_____   _____   _____

_____   _____   _____

pond	house
castle	nest
kennel	hangar

☆ **Trace.**

Metre is a measure of length.

Litre is a measure of liquid.

☆ **Classify these things according to how they are measured. Draw the picture and write the word.**

milk   string   water   petrol   wood   buildings

litre   **metre**

ai

sail   _____

nail   _____

hail   _____

pain   _____

wait   _____

paid   _____

paint   _____

again   _____

Money

dollars   _____

cents   _____

Common words

find   _____

saw   _____

My words

_____   _____

Unit 18

Rain, rain go away.
Come again another day.

⭐ **Write a list word for each clue.**

Frozen drops of rain _____

Once more _____

Was given some money _____

You use a brush to put this on _____

The hard part at the end of your finger _____

⭐ **Match the list words to the shapes.**

38

☆ Write the words.

paint
- s _____
- ed _____
- ing _____

wait
- s _____
- ed _____
- ing _____

☆ Fill the gap with <u>saw</u> and <u>sore</u>.

I _____ Jenny's _____ hand. It was bleeding.

☆ Circle the words with the same sound as <u>i</u> as in <u>find</u>.
Write the words on the line.

| find | pin | kind | behind | spring | wild | tip |
| little | in | blind | mind | this | fifty | tiger |

_____

☆ Put these words in sentences.

find _____

behind _____

☆ Write <u>cents</u> or <u>dollars</u>.

10 _____   90 _____   200 _____

95 _____   50 _____   15,000 _____

☆ Draw pictures for <u>sail</u> and <u>sale</u>. Use your dictionary to help you.

Unit 19 Review

⭐ **Complete the words.**

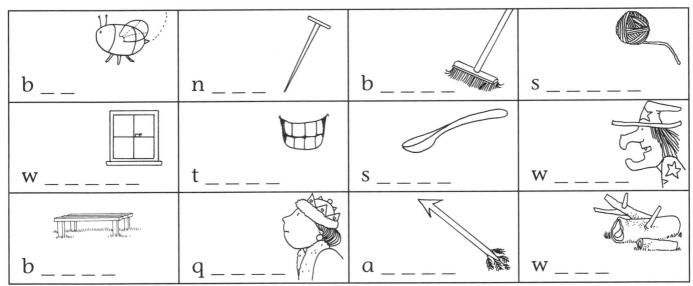

b _ _	n _ _ _	b _ _ _ _	s _ _ _ _ _
w _ _ _ _ _	t _ _ _ _	s _ _ _ _	w _ _ _ _ _
b _ _ _ _	q _ _ _ _	a _ _ _ _ _	w _ _ _

⭐ **Write the small words in:**

find   where   want   peach

_____   _____   _____   _____

_____   _____   _____   _____

_____

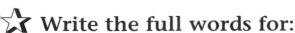

⭐ **Write the full words for:**

I'm = _____   didn't = _____

it's = _____   can't = _____

couldn't = _____   wouldn't = _____

⭐ **Choose the correct word from the box.**

1 I am _____ to the doctor in

    the _____.

2 We _____ told to _____ our

    lunches in the box.

put
going
morning
were

40

⭐ **Choose the correct letters from the circles to complete each word. Draw a picture for each word.**

(ng) (oo) (ee) (ea) (ch) (ai) (ow)

bun _ _	bl _ _	h _ _ k	sl _ _ p
p _ _ nt	stro _ _	sch _ _ l	t _ _ cher

⭐ **a or an?**

_____ kitten   _____ arrow   _____ ice-cream

_____ oval   _____ flower   _____ koala

⭐ **Write each word from the box next to the word below that sounds the same.**

here	which	too	saw	week
would	be	where	meet

to _____   meat _____   sore _____

hear _____   witch _____   wear _____

wood _____   bee _____   weak _____

⭐ **Circle the correct word.**

sail sale	which witch	meat meet
wood would	too two	flower flour

A Homophone Crossword

⭐ Complete the crossword using these homophones.

there	their
they're	hear
here	two
to	too
pair	pear
blue	blew
eight	ate
meet	meat
flower	flour
sale	sail
which	witch

Across

2 I _____ out the candles.

5 2 × 4 = _____

7 "Please come _____."

8 Use plain _____ in the cake.

9 He had a _____ on the yacht.

12 The ugly _____ made a spell.

15 She bought a _____ of shoes.

16 They put on _____ coats.

17 We live over _____.

18 We went _____ the shops.

19 She had _____ dollars to spend.

Down

1 _____ me at the shops.

2 The sky is _____ today.

3 _____ team came first?

4 A _____ is good to eat.

6 Did you _____ what I said.

8 That's a pretty _____.

10 Toby _____ his lunch.

11 _____ going to the zoo.

13 Our car is for _____.

14 They took _____ for a barbecue.

16 It was _____ wet to play outside.

17 We went _____ the shops.

A Sport Report

⭐ **Write the words with their different endings.**

Add **s**

Add **ed**

Add **ing**

play	_____	_____	_____
kick	_____	_____	_____
jump	_____	_____	_____
train	_____	_____	_____
yell	_____	_____	_____
start	_____	_____	_____
shout	_____	_____	_____
climb	_____	_____	_____
walk	_____	_____	_____
pull	_____	_____	_____

⭐ **Write a word from the exercise above for each clue.**

1 He _____ up the ropes.

2 They had footy _____ later.

3 She can _____ very loudly.

4 Jan went _____ around the lake.

5 He _____ out, "Help!"

6 The race _____ on time.

7 Can you _____ the tree?

8 Tom _____ 3 kms to his friend's house.

9 He _____ cricket every Saturday.

10 She was _____ the ropes.

The mystery word is _____

oa

road   _____

load   _____

toad   _____

loaf   _____

cloak   _____

toast   _____

float   _____

coach   _____

Breakfast time

eggs   _____

bacon   _____

Common words

when   _____

fast   _____

My words

_____   _____

Unit 21

Bacon and eggs on toast
is my kind of breakfast.

⭐ Trace and add <u>oa</u>
to each word.

⭐ Use the code to find the list words.

o	d	r
t		a
l	s	f

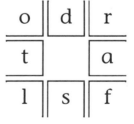

⭐ **Write the smaller words in:**

when   _____   _____

⭐ **Fill the gaps with <u>When</u>.**

_____ do elephants paint their toenails different colours?

_____ they want to hide in a Smarties packet.

⭐ **Fill the spaces with the word <u>fast</u>.**
Choose a picture and draw it under the correct words.

_ _ _ _ _   _ _ _ _ _er   _ _ _ _ _est

⭐ **Write a list word for each clue to find the mystery word.**
1 Meat from a pig
2 A place where cars go
3 "_____ will you be home?"
4 This looks like a frog
5 A witch might wear one
6 To rest on top of water
7 Someone who trains people in sport
8 Hens lay these
9 A cooked piece of bread

⭐ **Put the mystery word in a sentence.**

_____

or

born _____

torn _____

torch _____

corner _____

more _____

sore _____

horse _____

score _____

In the stable

foal _____

pony _____

Common words

forty _____

before _____

My words

_____ _____

The basketball **score** was **forty** to nineteen.

☆ **Circle the words that have <u>or</u> in them. Write them in the torch.**

star

know

more

town

torch

row

born

smart

corner

before

brown

torn

sore

toast

crown

score

forty

horse

☆ **Fill the gap with a list word.**

1 The _____ was eating some grass.

2 When Jessie fell over she had a _____ knee.

3 Could I please have some _____ cake?

4 Thirty plus ten equals _____.

5 Remember to wash your hands _____ you eat.

6 The chair was in the _____ of the room.

7 I use a _____ to see in the dark.

★ Change one letter in each word to make a new word.

1 Change **porch** to a small light. _____

2 Change **house** to an animal with a mane. _____

3 Change **horn** to something that is ripped. _____

4 Change **move** to a bigger amount. _____

5 Change **some** to a painful injury. _____

6 Change **scare** to points won in a game. _____

7 Change **fool** to a baby horse. _____

8 Change **pond** to a small horse. _____

★ Rewrite the list words by adding the vowels (<u>a e i o u</u>).

mr   frty   trch   sr

_____   _____   _____   _____

crnr   pny   brn   fl

_____   _____   _____   _____

★ Put these words in sentences.

before _____

forty _____

foal _____

Wordsearch → ← ↓ ↑ ✓

★ Colour each list word in a different colour. Write each word on the lines.

_____

_____

_____

_____

t	s	c	o	r	e	a	e
y	n	o	p	j	d	i	c
t	o	r	c	h	b	e	h
r	f	n	r	o	t	r	m
o	g	e	f	r	n	o	k
f	e	r	o	s	r	f	j
q	c	j	a	e	o	e	c
a	m	i	l	p	b	b	z

ll, ss, tt, nn

sell _____

bell _____

doll _____

cross _____

press _____

little _____

butter _____

funny _____

Let's laugh

joke _____

riddle _____

Common words

called _____

hello _____

My words

_____ _____

 Write the words.

call ⟨ s _____
      ed _____
      ing _____

Here is a **riddle**.
Q. Why did the chicken **cross** the playground?
A. To get to the other slide.

☆ Colour all the spaces with a double-letter word to find the shape of a list word.

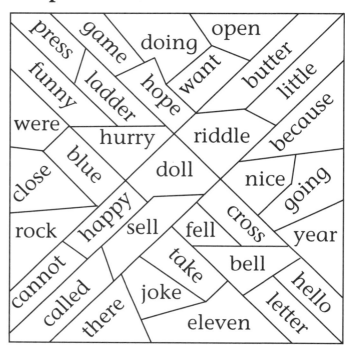

The shape of the list word is a

_____.

☆ Write the double-letter words that you have coloured.

_____

_____

_____

_____

☆ **Underline the correct word.**

1 I like (better, butter) on my toast.

2 My mother was very (cross, press) when I broke the window.

3 The teacher will (hello, press) the button to make the school (sell, bell) ring.

☆ **If a word ends in <u>ss</u>, <u>ch</u>, <u>sh</u>, or <u>x</u>, add <u>es</u> to make it plural.**

kiss _____kisses_____   dress _____

brush _____   bunch _____

cross _____   fox _____

wish _____   peach _____

☆ **Draw three meanings for the word <u>cross</u>.**

☆ **Use the code to read the riddle.**

a	b	c	d	e	f	g	h	i	j	k	l	m	n	o	p	q	r	s	t	u	v	w	x	y	z
1	2	3	4	5	6	7	8	9	10	11	12	13	14	15	16	17	18	19	20	21	22	23	24	25	26

Q. 23 8 1 20   7 15 5 19   21 16   1 14 4   23 15 2 2 12 5 19?

_____

A. 1   10 5 12 12 25 3 15 16 20 5 18.

_____

49

dd, pp, bb, rr

teddy _____

cuddle _____

happy _____

puppy _____

bubble _____

rabbit _____

sorry _____

hurry _____

Friendship

kind _____

friend _____

Common words

bigger _____

biggest _____

My words

_____ _____

Unit 24

A **friend** in need is a **friend** indeed.

⭐ Write the double-letter words inside the teddy.

teddy   down   funny   rabbit

apple   carrot

friend   want

puppy   happy

now

they   kind

sorry   nine

paper   hope

⭐ Write the list words.

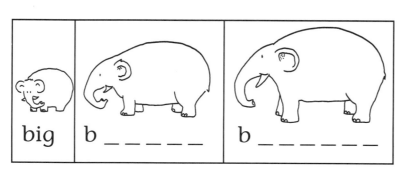

big   b _ _ _ _ _   b _ _ _ _ _ _

_ _ _ _ _ _   _ _ _ _ _

_ _ _ _ _ _   _ _ _ _ _ _

50

☆ **Write a list word for each clue.**

1 A baby dog
2 A ball of air
3 A mate
4 Glad
5 Soft toy bear
6 Feeling sad about something
7 Rush
8 Hug
9 An animal like a hare
10 Helpful and caring

1				■
2				
3				
4				■
5				■
6				■
7				■
8				
9				
10			■	

☆ **Use double letters from the bubbles to complete each word. Draw a line from each word to its matching picture.**

(dd)   (rr)   (bb)   (pp)

ra ___ ___ it

bu ___ ___ le

ha ___ ___ y

che ___ ___ y

la ___ ___ er

a ___ ___ le

ca ___ ___ ot

pu ___ ___ le

☆ **Change one letter to make a new word. There is a clue in the brackets.**

cuddle _____
(a small pool of water)

flipper _____
(a soft indoor shoe)

berry _____
(a boat)

riddle _____
(half way)

OU

out   _____

our   _____

loud   _____

house   _____

mouse   _____

shout   _____

count   _____

round   _____

Numbers

hundred   _____

thousand   _____

Common words

found   _____

about   _____

My words

_____   _____

Unit 25

Can you **count** to one **hundred**?
_____

Can you **count** to one **thousand**? _____

☆ **Label each picture with a list word.**

☆ **Fill the gap with <u>hour</u> or <u>our</u>.**

1   We took _____ dog to the vet.

2   Our grade went swimming for one _____.

☆ **Write the parts of the compound words.**

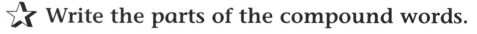

without = _____ + _____

lighthouse = _____ + _____

☆ **Help the mouse find his house by writing the list word for each clue.**

yell

a small animal

belonging to us

a home

one

1000

noisy

like a ball

discovered

not in

☆ **Write these words in alphabetical order.**

1 cloud   round   about   mouth

_____

2 thousand   sound   proud   loud

_____

3 our   around   mouse   house

_____

☆ **Rewrite the number words with their vowels. (a, e, i, o, u)**

hndrd   thsnd   fv   twnty

_____   _____   _____   _____

ght   tw   fftn   fr

_____   _____   _____   _____

air

air _____

hair _____

fair _____

pair _____

chair _____

fairy _____

Make-believe

magic _____

wishes _____

Common words

ask _____

asked _____

who _____

than _____

My words

_____ _____

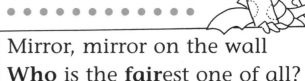

Unit 26

Mirror, mirror on the wall
Who is the **fair**est one of all?

⭐ **Write the words.**

a + i + r = _____

p + air = _____

f + air = _____

f + air + y = _____

h + air = _____

ch + air = _____

⭐ **Label the pictures.**

_____   _____

_____   _____

⭐ **Write the parts of the compound words.**

haircut = _____ + _____

airport = _____ + _____

⭐ **Fill the gap with <u>pear</u> or <u>pair</u>.**

1 I have a new _____ of shoes.

2 He had an apple and a _____ for lunch.

54

☆ **Write the words.**

ask ⟨ s _____
      ed _____
      ing _____

wish ⟨ es _____
       ed _____
       ing _____

☆ **Help the magician unjumble the sentences.**

1 is than My Kim's hair. longer hair

    My _____

2 of pair thongs. new lost Shaun his

    Shaun _____

3 magic The granted wishes. three fairy

    The _____

4 sitting has Bear. "Who on Father chair?" been said my

    "Who _____

    _____

☆ **Use the list words to complete these puzzles.**

	f			
	a			
	i			
	r			

	w		
	i		
	t		
	c		
	h		

☆ **Use the list word that would come between these words in a dictionary.**

1 broom _____ doll

2 near _____ round

3 goat _____ jump

4 kitten _____ open

aw

paw _____

jaw _____

raw _____

draw _____

claw _____

lawn _____

yawn _____

crawl _____

Wild animals

lion _____

tiger _____

Common words

most _____

both _____

My words

_____   _____

The **lion** and **tiger both** use their large **paws** and **claws**.

⭐ **Write the list words for the clues.**

1 An animal's nail

_____

2 Not cooked

_____

3 Make a picture

_____

4 Move on hands and feet

_____

5 Part of your head

_____

6 An animal's foot

_____

7 Grass

_____

8 Nearly all

_____

10 Take a deep breath

12 A striped animal

9 The two of them

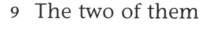

11 A large cat

_____

Draw a line between each word. Rewrite each sentence.

1 Most/childrenliketodraw.

_____

2 Thebabycrawledoverthelawn.

_____

3 Thelionheldtherawmeatwithbothclaws.

_____

_____

 Fill each gap with a word from the box.

1 Our cat has a sore _____.

2 Can you hear the _____ of the lions?

3 I will _____ the milk for you.

4 Jim likes to eat _____ vegetables.

raw

roar

paw

pour

⭐ **Circle the odd word. Write it on the line.**

draw	paint	write	crawl	_____
crow	tiger	hawk	owl	_____
draw	run	walk	crawl	_____
snake	lion	lizard	goanna	_____
lion	tiger	panther	claw	_____
paw	tail	lawn	head	_____
leg	paw	foot	straw	_____
jump	kick	yawn	hop	_____
saw	puff	blow	yawn	_____
zero	most	none	nothing	_____

ew

few	_____
flew	_____
grew	_____
drew	_____
blew	_____
knew	_____
new	_____

Flight

plane	_____
high	_____

Common words

does	_____
once	_____

My words

_____   _____

The aero**plane** flew **high** up through the clouds.

☆ **Complete the list words. Write each word on the line.**

new   few

_____   _____

blew   grew

_____   _____

once   high

_____   _____

flew   drew

_____   _____

☆ **Fill the gap with <u>new</u> or <u>knew</u>.**
Example:
I have a <u>new</u> dress.
He <u>knew</u> how to ride a bike.

1 The dog _____ the way home.

2 My father has a _____ car.

☆ **Fill the gap with <u>blew</u> or <u>blue</u> (a colour).**

I _____ up the _____ balloon.

⭐ **Colour the correct boxes.**

1 My little brother | drew | knew | on the wall.

2 During the storm, the wind | drew | blew |
a big branch off the tree.

3 We feed our cat | does | once | a day.

4 I have only a | flew | few | lollies left.

5 The | plane | plain | | flew | few |
over the sea.

6 Where | does | blew | your mother work?

7 Jack's beanstalk | new | grew |
| high | does | up into the clouds.

⭐ **Write the words that you coloured.**

_____

_____

⭐ **Write an <u>ew</u> word from the list.**

1 Today I grow, yesterday I _____ .

2 Today I blow, yesterday I _____ .

3 Today I draw, yesterday I _____ .

⭐ **Use a dictionary to complete the following.**

1 The word after **few** is _____ .

2 The word after **once** is _____ .

3 The word that comes before **high** is _____ .

4 The word that comes before **new** is _____ .

5 The second word after **grew** is _____ .

Unit 29 Review

⭐ **Circle the correct word.**

Cameron (new, knew) he was getting a surprise for his birthday. It was a (new, knew) puppy.

⭐ **Fill each gap with a word from the box.**

about
who   asked
than   fast
found

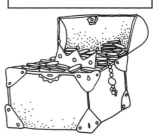

1 A rocket is __ __ __ __ e r

  __ __ __ __ a snail.

2 "__ __ __ will help us dig a hole?"

  __ __ __ __ __ Nick.

3 The pirates __ __ __ __ __ out

  __ __ __ __ __ the hidden treasure.

⭐ **Choose ll, ss, tt, dd, pp, bb, rr to make the words.**

li __ __ le   cu __ __ le   so __ __ y   pre __ __ __

se __ __   bu __ __ er   he __ __ o

hu __ __ y   cro __ __   ha __ __ y

⭐ **Trace the words and draw a picture for each word.**

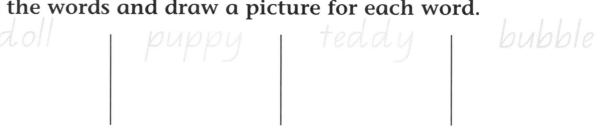

doll   puppy   teddy   bubble

⭐ **Trace and add es to the words. Draw the pictures.**

one witch   three witch___

one box   four box___

A "which word" quiz

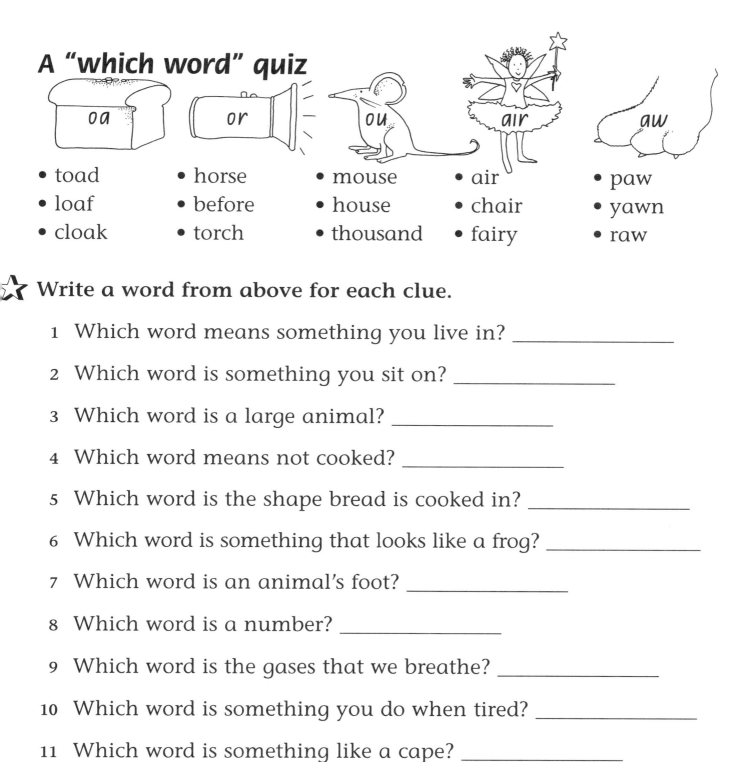

oa
- toad
- loaf
- cloak

or
- horse
- before
- torch

ou
- mouse
- house
- thousand

air
- air
- chair
- fairy

aw
- paw
- yawn
- raw

⭐ **Write a word from above for each clue.**

1 Which word means something you live in? _____

2 Which word is something you sit on? _____

3 Which word is a large animal? _____

4 Which word means not cooked? _____

5 Which word is the shape bread is cooked in? _____

6 Which word is something that looks like a frog? _____

7 Which word is an animal's foot? _____

8 Which word is a number? _____

9 Which word is the gases that we breathe? _____

10 Which word is something you do when tired? _____

11 Which word is something like a cape? _____

12 Which word is the opposite to after? _____

13 Which word is something you use in the dark? _____

14 Which word is a magical person in stories? _____

15 Which word is an animal that likes cheese? _____

Unit 30 Stepping up

Rhyme time

☆ Write each word from the box underneath the word that it rhymes with.

share	drawn	grass	threw
door	roast	middle	ground

toast   score   pass   riddle

_____   _____   _____   _____

sound   pair   yawn   grew

_____   _____   _____   _____

Doing a jig

☆ Make eight compound words by matching the jigsaw pieces with a line. Write the compound words on the lines below.

score	news		paper	word
chair	out		post	board
horse	round	+	lift	about
goal	cross		side	shoe

_____   _____   _____   _____

_____   _____   _____   _____

Compound list

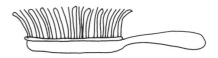

⭐ Make a list of compound words with the word 'hair' in them.

_____

Make a list of compound words with the word 'shoe' in them.

_____

You be the editor

⭐ Con has made a new menu for his cafe. However, he has made sixteen spelling mistakes. Circle them and write them correctly on the lines below.

Con's Cafe

Brekfast Menu		Lunch Menu	
bakon and egs	3.00	sandwitches:	
toastd sandwich	2.20	salad	2.20
appel muffins	1.50	meet	2.50
toast with buter	1.50	cheesse	2.20
tea	1.00	hot dog	2.00
coffee	1.20	pie	2.20
drinks	1.00	milk shake	1.50

Dinner Menu

fish and chips	2.50	salad	2.00
hamburga	2.80	fride rice	1.50
roast chiken	3.50	jellie	1.20
pize – won slice	2.00	ice-creem	1.20

_____

_____

_____

⭐ Write the items you would order from the dinner menu if you had $6.00 to spend. _____

63

ir

girl _____

stir _____

bird _____

first _____

third _____

shirt _____

dirty _____

birthday _____

Birthdays

present _____

invite _____

Common words

twenty _____

thirty _____

My words

_____ _____

Your **dirty shirt** will be **first** in the wash!

⭐ Write list words for the pictures.

_____

10+10 _____

_____

_____

_____

3X10 _____

⭐ Use the code to find the list words.

d	t	r
s	y	b
f	i	h

☆ **Fill the gaps with a list word or one from the box. Use the picture clues to help you.**

buttons
stars lace
fairy

It was Claire's birthday. She was very excited

as her friends were coming at three 30 _ _ _ _ _ _

for a party. The 1st _ _ _ _ _ _ present she opened

was a pretty _ _ _ _ _ _ with _ _ _ _ _

and _ _ _ _ _ _ _ _ down the front. The second

_ _ _ _ _ _ _ was a toy _ _ _ _ _

that could sing. The 3rd _ _ _ _ _ _ present was a set

of _ _ _ _ _ _ wings with _ _ _ _ _ _

on them. What a lucky _ _ _ _ _ she was!

☆ **Answer first, second or third.**

1 Which dog has spots? _____

2 Which dog has a black tip on its tail? _____

3 Which dog is the smallest dog? _____

4 Which dog has the longest tail? _____

5 Which dog has a black nose? _____

6 Which dog has the longest ears? _____

☆ **Put these words in sentences.**

present _____

invite _____

y

very   _____

only   _____

any   _____

many   _____

lady   _____

baby   _____

ugly   _____

jelly   _____

Numbers

seventy   _____

eighty   _____

Common words

fifty   _____

sixty   _____

My words

_____   _____

Unit 32

Jelly can be very wobbly.

⭐ Colour over the x's and rewrite the letters that are left to find a list word.

xxaxnxy   _____

lxaxdxxy   _____

xbxabxyx   _____

xvxexryx   _____

fixxfxty   _____

mxaxxnxy   _____

sevxenty   _____

xxoxnlyx   _____

exigxhty   _____

⭐ Find the small words in:

lady _____   only _____

many _____ _____ _____

⭐ Write a list word for these clues.

1 Soft wobbly food ☐☐☐☐ y

2 A very young child ☐☐☐ y

3 Not pretty to look at ☐☐☐ y

4 A large number of things ☐☐☐ y

5 An elephant is _____ heavy. ☐☐☐ y

☆ **Write the words on the lines.**

body _____

one _____

thing _____

any thing _____

where _____

how _____

way _____

☆ **Write the answers in number words.**

1 Ten more than fifty equals _____.

2 Forty plus forty equals _____.

3 Half of one hundred equals _____.

4 Eighty take away ten equals _____.

5 Ten less than ninety equals _____.

6 Thirty plus twenty equals _____.

☆ **If the y sounds like the y in jelly, write the word in the jelly.**
If the y sounds like the y in fry write the word in the frypan.

ugly   cry   very   dry   sky   baby   sixty
fly   by   many   my   any   try

☆ **Write the list words in alphabetical order.**

_____

_____

er

over _____

sister _____

winter _____

water _____

clever _____

finger _____

other _____

monster _____

Family words

mother _____

father _____

Common words

after _____

your _____

My words

_____   _____

Be **clever** and don't waste **water**. Turn **your** taps off **after** using them.

☆ **Write a list word for each clue.**

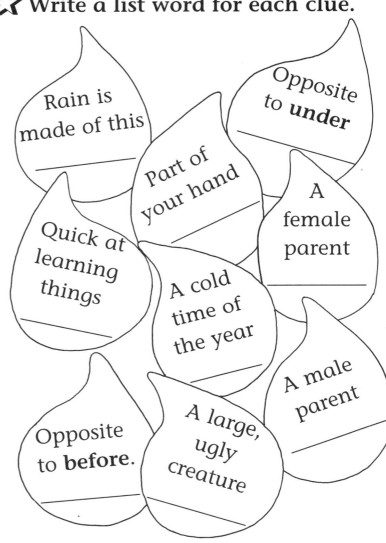

Rain is made of this _____

Opposite to **under** _____

Part of your hand _____

Quick at learning things _____

A female parent _____

A cold time of the year _____

A male parent _____

Opposite to **before**. _____

A large, ugly creature _____

☆ **Write the list words that have these words in them.**

is _*sister*_   on _____   the _____

our _____   fat _____   _____

win _____   fin _____

ever _____   moth _____

☆ **Colour the correct box.**

1 When is [your | you] birthday?

2 Spring comes [before | after] winter.

☆ **Write the compound words.**

after + noon = _____   your + self = _____

☆ **Trace and add er. Draw the pictures.**

riv ___ ___ ___   flow ___ ___ ___

pap ___ ___ ___   numb ___ ___ ___

ladd ___ ___ ___   butt ___ ___ ___

spid ___ ___ ___   tig ___ ___ ___

☆ **Help the monster unjumble the sentences.**

1 mother party? to going Are the father your and

_____

_____

2 made the a spider under clever flowers. The web

_____

_____

3 over water. My falling the sister in crossed the without river

_____

_____

☆ **Look up monster in the dictionary. Write out its meaning.**

_____

☆ **On a piece of paper draw the ugliest monster you can.**

ur

turn _____

burn _____

hurt _____

curl _____

surf _____

nurse _____

purse _____

church _____

Hospitals

doctor _____

Dr _____

Common words

next _____

why _____

My words

_____ _____

Unit 34

Next time you go to the **surf** remember to use a sunscreen so that you don't get sun**burn**.

☆ **Fill the purse with <u>ur</u> coins. Write the words in the purse.**

storm   clue   blue
purse
torn   for   surf
turn
sport   hurt
nurse
burn   true   glue   church
curl

a b c d e f g h i j k l m n o p q r s t u v w x y z

☆ **Write list words that start with the letter that comes after:**

s *t* _____   m _____   b _____   c _____

a _____   m _____   b _____   c _____

g _____   o _____   v _____

⭐ **Complete the table.**

	Add **s**	Add **ed**	Add **ing**
turn	_____	_____	_____
curl	_____	_____	_____
burn	_____	_____	_____

⭐ **Write a list word for each clue to find the mystery word.**

1 To move around; twist
2 A building where people go to pray
3 A person who looks after sick people
4 The waves on the sea
5 The full word for Dr
6 A place to put your money
7 To make something feel pain
8 The one after this one
9 To be on fire

The mystery word is

_____

Abbreviations

An abbreviation is the shortening of a word.

⭐ **Write the abbreviation next to the matching full word.**

Vic.   Rd   P.O.   St
Mr   kg.   Dr   P.T.O.

Doctor _____   Road _____

Street _____   Post Office _____

Mister _____   Please turn over _____

kilogram _____   Victoria _____

ea

head   _____

dead   _____

bread   _____

wear   _____

heavy   _____

read   _____

Weight

gram   _____

kilogram   _____

Common words

push   _____

pull   _____

work   _____

word   _____

My words

_____   _____

Unit 35

Wear your helmet to protect your head.

☆ **Unjumble the list words.**

_____   _____

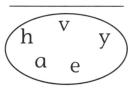   

_____   _____

     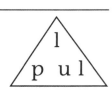

_____   _____

     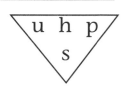

_____   _____

_____

☆ **Use the word <u>read</u> to complete these sentences.**

1 Today I will _____ this book.

2 Yesterday I _____ that book.

Read each sentence aloud.

Does <u>read</u> sound the same in each sentence? _____

72

☆ Circle the words where the **ea** sounds like
the **ea** in **bread**. Write them inside the bread.

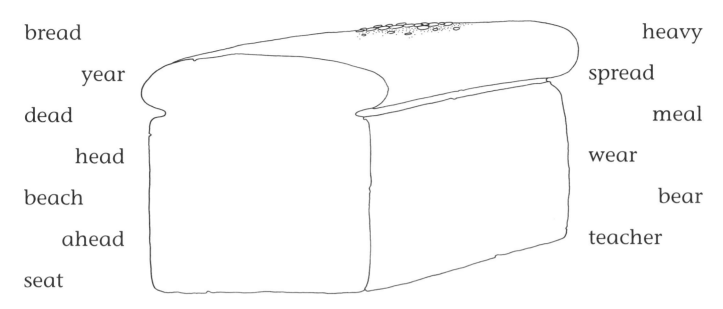

bread

year

dead

head

beach

ahead

seat

heavy

spread

meal

wear

bear

teacher

☆ Circle the word that does not rhyme. Write it on the line.

1	work	gram	ham	pram	_____
2	ball	pull	call	fall	_____
3	brush	rush	push	hush	_____
4	word	cord	bored	lord	_____
5	hear	bear	dear	fear	_____
6	word	bird	heard	bread	_____

☆ Write grams or kilograms.

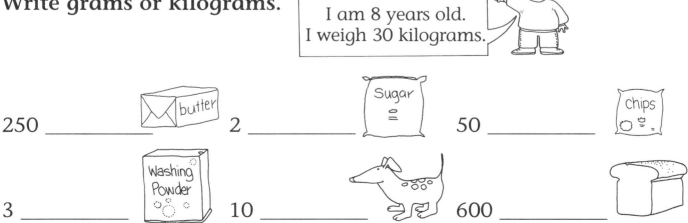

I am 8 years old.
I weigh 30 kilograms.

250 _____   butter   2 _____   Sugar   50 _____   chips

3 _____   Washing Powder   10 _____   600 _____

oi

join _____

coin _____

oil _____

point _____

noise _____

Sounds

noisy _____

quiet _____

Common words

use _____

used _____

people

place _____

My words

_____ _____

People have **used coin**s as money for thousands of years.

⭐ **Match list words to the shapes.**

⭐ **Write each line of words in alphabetical order.**

1 used   point   coin   join

_____

2 noise   quiet   people   oil

_____

3 place   soil   use   noisy

_____

☆ **Rewrite these sentences using the correct word.**
 1 The children were very (quite, quiet)
    while they listened to the story.

 _____

 _____

 2 Donna (use, used) glue to (join, coin) the pieces of wood.

 _____

 _____

 3 The (people, point) next to our (please, place) had a
    (noise, noisy) party last night.

 _____

 _____

☆ **Write your new words on the lines.**

 use $\Big<$ s   _____   join $\Big<$ s   _____
         d   _____   ed _____
                                    ing _____

☆ **Find twelve oi words in the wordsearch.**
 Write them on the lines.

 → ← ↓ ↑ ↗ ↘

b	b	c	e	g	p	o	i	n	t
j	s	o	l	j	o	k	o	f	o
o	p	i	i	c	i	i	d	o	i
i	o	l	o	l	s	s	o	i	l
n	i	l	d	e	o	n	a	l	e
h	l	c	o	i	n	p	l	m	t

 _____ _____

 _____ _____

 _____ _____

 _____ _____

 _____ _____

 _____ _____

ay

days _____

away _____

today _____

Monday _____

Tuesday _____

Wednesday _____

Thursday _____

Friday _____

The weekend

Saturday _____

Sunday _____

Common words

played _____

playing _____

My words

_____ _____

Unit 37

Rain, rain go **away**,
come again another **day**.
But not a **Saturday**
or a **Sunday**.

☆ **Complete the list words.
Write each word on the line.**

today   Monday

_____ _____

played   away

_____ _____

Friday   Tuesday

_____ _____

☆ **Write the words.**

play ⟨ s _____
        ed _____
        ing _____

☆ **Write the parts of the compound words.**

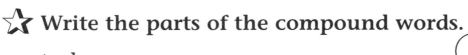

today = _____ + _____

birthday = _____ + _____

playground = _____ + _____

★ Write the day of the week.

The day after Monday is _____.

The day before Saturday is _____.

Two days after Monday is _____.

Two days before Saturday is _____.

Three days after Friday is _____.

The days of the weekend are _____
and _____.

★ Write the ay words.

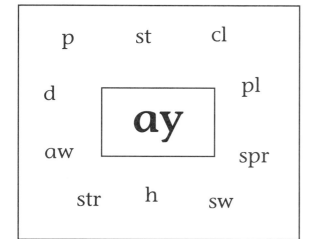

_____   _____

_____   _____

_____   _____

_____   _____

_____   _____

★ Complete the word puzzle.

My 1st letter is in heat but not in meat.   _____

My 2nd letter is in fox but not in fix.   _____

My 3rd letter is in look but not in book   _____

My 4th letter is in still but not in stall.   _____

My 5th letter is in day but not in say.   _____

My 6th letter is in last but not in lost.   _____

My 7th letter is in tray but not in trap.   _____

What word am I? _____

o

son   _____

some   _____

come   _____

done   _____

none   _____

love   _____

honey   _____

money   _____

My moneybox

full   _____

empty   _____

Common words

above   _____

front   _____

My words

_____   _____

Unit 38

Save **some** of your **money** and soon your **money**box will be **full**.

Rhyming words

⭐ Choose a list word.

s
o
n

a b o v e

s o m e

b u l l

h o n e y

h u n t

⭐ Write the parts of the compound words.

someone = _____ + _____

somewhere = _____ + _____

⭐ Write <u>sun</u> or <u>son</u>  .

1 Mrs Smith took her
_____ to the doctor.

2 Keep out of the _____
on a hot day.

⭐ **Write a list word for each clue.**

1 Not any

2 Coins and notes

3 Like very much

4 Sticky food made by bees

5 Nothing inside

6 Filled up

7 Over

8 A few

1				■
2				
3				■
4				
5				
6			■	
7				
8			■	

⭐ **Write a list word that is opposite to each word.**

back _____

all _____

hate _____

below _____

go _____

daughter _____

⭐ **Drop the e and add ing.**
Example: com$\not{e}$ coming

love _____

use _____

smile _____

bake _____

hide _____

save _____

joke _____

hope _____

⭐ **Change a letter to make a new word. Read the clues.**

none   _____ (a part of your face)

come   _____ (where you live)

full   _____ (the male of cattle)

Unit 39

en

even _____

oven _____

seven _____

taken _____

chicken _____

children _____

seventeen _____

In the oven

bake _____

roast _____

Common words

sixteen _____

eighteen _____

My words

_____ _____

Mum has **taken** the roast **chicken** out of the **oven**.

☆ **Write the list words.**

_____

 18

_____

17 16

_____ _____

☆ **Write <u>odd</u> or <u>even</u> for these numbers.**

8 _____   19 _____

7 _____   14 _____

☆ **Circle the words that rhyme with <u>bake</u>.**

cake   oven   take   lake   made   make   joke   snake

☆ **Circle the words that rhyme with <u>roast</u>.**

fast   most   toast   cost   post   coast

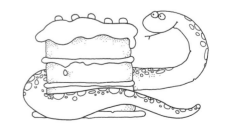

80

A *number* crossword

☆ Write a number word for each clue.

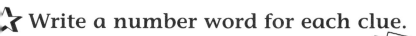

Across

1 15 + 2 =

2 2 × 2 =

4 9 + 9 =

6 3 × 3 =

8 10 + 5 =

10 8 + 8 =

11 10 − 8 =

12 2 × 10 =

13 20 − 10 =

Down

1 10 − 3 =

3 1 × 1 =

5 10 + 3 =

6 9 × 10 =

7 9 + 2 =

9 20 + 10 + 10 =

☆ Write the small words in:

taken _____   children _____   open _____   garden _____

☆ Write <u>children</u> and <u>taken</u> into one sentence.

_____

_____

☆ How many number words can you find?
Write them.

_____

_____

81

Unit 40 Review

⭐ Complete the words.

b _ _ _	f _ _ _ _	l _ _ _	c _ _ _ _ _ _ _
s _ _ _ _	n _ _ _ _ _	t _ _ _ _	s _ _ _ _ _ _
e _ _ _ _ _ _ _	f _ _ _ _ _	c _ _ _ _ _ _ _ _	m _ _ _ _ _

⭐ Write the smaller words in:

join	bread	dirty	your	water
_____	_____	_____	_____	_____
mother	many	none	_____	_____
_____	_____	_____	used	money
_____	_____	_____	_____	_____
_____	_____	_____	_____	_____

⭐ Write the part of the compound words.

birthday = _____ + _____   fireplace = _____ + _____

ladybird = _____ + _____   playtime = _____ + _____

⭐ Write the opposites. Use words from the box.

before _____   back _____

push _____   odd _____

below _____   noisy _____

front	
quiet	after
pull	above
	even

82

☆ Choose the correct letters to complete each word.
Draw a picture for each word.

(er) (y) (ir) (ur) (oi) (o) (ea) (ay)

g __ __ l	ch __ __ ch	h __ __ vy	pl __ __
wat __ __	h __ ney	lad __	c __ __ n

☆ Drop the e and add ing.

make   *making*   ride   _____

come   _____   live   _____

take   _____   hope   _____

☆ Write the full words for:

Dr = _____   Rd = _____   kg. = _____

Mr = _____   St = _____   gm = _____

☆ Write the words for the pictures.

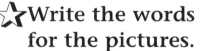

s _ _ _ _   p _ _ _ _ _ _

k _ _ _   c _ _ _ _ _ _

b _ _ _ _   j _ _ _ _

b _ _ _   f _ _ _ _ _ _

f _ _ _ _   t _ _ _ _ _

l _ _ _   c _ _ _ _

Measurements

 Write the measurements from the box under the correct pictures.

second	gram	minute	kilometre
litre	metre	kilogram	hour

_____ _____ _____ _____

_____ _____ _____

_____

Subtract a letter

Subtract one letter to make a new word. Match the new word to its clue with a line. The first one has been done for you.

1 many	man	part of the face
2 eighty	_____	not odd
3 noise	_____	give up
4 read	_____	a male
5 mice	_____	the rich part of milk
6 know	_____	level
7 scream	_____	frozen water
8 float	_____	four plus four
9 quilt	_____	a colour
10 seven	_____	at this time

Write your own words where you can subtract one letter to make a new word.

Puzzle Page

⭐ Match two boxes to find eight animals. Write them on the lines.

bab	pos	bit	bat
key	mag	pig	mon
pyt	rab	oon	sum
let	wom	hon	pie

_____   _____

_____   _____

_____   _____

_____   _____

⭐ Change one letter at a time to make a new word. The first one has been done for you.

l	o	v	e
l	o	s	e
l	o	s	t
p	o	s	t
p	a	s	t

b	a	k	e .
c	o	s	t

c	o	m	e
t	u	r	n

f	u	l	l
b	e	a	t

⭐ Write a word to match the picture clues to find the mystery word.

p	a	r			
p	a	r			
p	a	r			
p	a	r			
p	a	r			
p	a	r			

The mystery word is _____.

Alphabetical list

A a
about
above
after
again
air
along
animal
any
apple
arrow
ask
asked
away

B b
baby
backyard
bacon
bake
bang
bark
basketball
because
bee
before
bell
belong
bench
bigger
biggest
bike
bird
birthday
blew
blow
blue
bone
boots
born
both
bowl

bread
broom
brush
bubble
bunch
burn
butter

C c
cake
called
came
carpet
cents
chair
cheer
chicken
children
chose
church
claw
clever
cloak
close
coach
coin
colour
come
computer
cone
cooking
cool
corner
could
count
crawl
cross
crowd
crown
crush
cuddle
curl

D d
dark
days
dead
deep
dirty
do
doctor
does
doing
doll
dollars
done
down
Dr
draw
drew
drove

E e
each
eggs
eighteen
eighty
eleven
empty
even

F f
fair
fairy
fast
father
feed
few
fifteen
fifty
find
finger
first
flew
float
flour

flower
foal
food
forty
found
fourteen
fresh
Friday
friend
front
frown
full
funny

G g
game
garden
girl
glow
going
goodbye
gram
grew
growl
grown

H h
hail
hair
half
happy
hard
head
hear
heavy
hello
here
high
home
honey
hood
hoof
hook

hope
horse
house
how
howl
hundred
hurry
hurt

I i
I'm
invite
it's

J j
jacket
jaw
jelly
join
joke

K k
kangaroo
kilogram
kind
kite
kitten
knew
know
koala

L l
lady
lamb
later
lawn
lion
litre
little
live
load
loaf
looked

loud
love

M m
made
magic
make
many
market
meal
meet
metre
mine
Monday
money
monster
more
morning
most
mother
mouse

N n
nail
name
near
neck
new
next
nice
nineteen
ninety
noise
noisy
none
note
now
nurse

O o
o'clock
oil
once
only
open
other

our
out
oven
over
own

P p
packet
paid
pain
paint
pair
paper
party
past
paw
peach
pear
pencil
people
pinch
place
plane
plant
played
playing
point
pony
present
press
pull
punch
puppy
purse
push
put

Q q
quack
queen
quiet

R r
rabbit
race
rang

raw
read
real
rice
riddle
ride
road
roast
roof
rope
round
runners

S s
sail
Saturday
saw
school
score
seat
sell
seven
seventeen
seventy
shape
shed
ship
shirt
shoe
shout
sister
sixteen
sixty
sleep
slide
slow
some
son
sore
sorry
spade
splash
spoon
sport
spring
start

stick
stir
stood
string
stripe
strong
stung
such
Sunday
surf

T t
take
taken
teacher
team
teddy
teeth
than
their
them
then
there
they
think
third
thirteen
thirty
this
thousand
throw
Thursday
tiger
toad
toast
today
too
torch
torn
track
truck
true
Tuesday
turn
twelve
twenty

U u
ugly
use
used

V v
very

W w
wait
want
water
wear
Wednesday
week
were
what
when
where
which
white
who
why
wild
window
winter
wishes
witch
with
woke
wood
word
work
would

Y y
yawn
year
your

Z z
zoo

OXFORD

UNIVERSITY PRESS

253 Normanby Road, South Melbourne, Victoria 3205, Australia

Oxford University Press is a department of the University of Oxford.
It furthers the University's objective of excellence in research,
scholarship, and education by publishing worldwide in

Oxford New York
Auckland Cape Town Dar es Salaam Hong Kong
Karachi Kuala Lumpur Madrid Melbourne Mexico City Nairobi
New Delhi Shanghai Taipei Toronto

With offices in
Argentina Austria Brazil Chile Czech Republic France Greece
Guatemala Hungary Italy Japan Poland Portugal Singapore
South Korea Switzerland Thailand Turkey Ukraine Vietnam

OXFORD is a trade mark of Oxford University Press in the UK and in
certain other countries

ISBN 978 0 19 555314 7
ISBN 0 19 555314 4

Illustrations by Annie White
Typeset by Alena Jencik, Grand Graphix Pty Ltd
Printed in Hong Kong by Sheck Wah Tong Printing Press Ltd